BOA
EDITIONS LTD

THE BOOK OF THINGS

T0163988

Kamen

Nihče ne sliši, kar brani kamen v sebi:
nematno, le njegovo je, kot bolečina
ujeta med usnje čevlja in podplat.

Ko jo netuješ, nenstrmi listje v goloti
kar je bilo, ne bo nikoli več,
in kupi dngih znamenj v tkolmenju.
Vonj bližnjih ambulant. Nemgui napuj.

Kar branist v seli, ne sliši milša.
Edini prekvalec mojega kam na ni.
Pravzan ni ga odušel.

THE BOOK OF THINGS

POEMS BY

ALEŠ ŠTEGER

TRANSLATED FROM THE SLOVENIAN BY

BRIAN HENRY

BOA EDITIONS, LTD. ☙ ROCHESTER, NY ❧ 2010

First Edition
10 11 12 13   7 6 5 4 3 2 1

For information about permission to reuse any material from this book, please contact The Permissions Company at www.permissionscompany.com or e-mail permdude@eclipse.net.

Publications by BOA Editions, Ltd.—a not-for-profit corporation under section 501 (c) (3) of the United States Internal Revenue Code—are made possible with funds from a variety of sources, including public funds from the New York State Council on the Arts, a state agency; the Literature Program of the National Endowment for the Arts; the County of Monroe, NY; the Lannan Foundation for support of the Lannan Translations Selection Series; the Sonia Raiziss Giop Charitable Foundation; the Mary S. Mulligan Charitable Trust; the Rochester Area Community Foundation; the Arts & Cultural Council for Greater Rochester; the Steeple-Jack Fund; the Ames-Amzalak Memorial Trust in memory of Henry Ames, Semon Amzalak and Dan Amzalak; and contributions from many individuals nationwide.

Cover Design: Sandy Knight
Cover Art: "Girl Art Iron and 3 Chairs" by Belinda Bryce
Interior Design and Composition: Richard Foerster
BOA Logo: Mirko

Library of Congress Cataloging-in-Publication Data

Šteger, Aleš.
[Knjiga stvari. English]
The book of things : poems / by Aleš Šteger ; [translated from the Slovenian by Brian Henry]. 1st ed.
    p. cm. — (Lannan translations selection series)
ISBN 978-1-934414-41-5
1. Šteger, Aleš—Translations into English. I. Henry, Brian, 1972– II. Title.
PG1919.29.T43K5813 2010
891.8'416—dc22

2010009198

NATIONAL
ENDOWMENT
FOR THE ARTS
A great nation
deserves great art.

BOA Editions, Ltd.
250 North Goodman Street, Suite 306
Rochester, NY 14607
www.boaeditions.org
A. Poulin, Jr., Founder (1938–1996)

State of the Arts

NYSCA

CONTENTS

A word does not exist for every thing.
—Slovenian dictionary

INTRODUCTION

From his first book of poems, *Šahovnice ur* (*Chessboards of Hours*), published in 1995 when he was twenty-two-years old, Aleš Šteger has been considered one of Slovenia's most promising poets. That promise has been unleashed over the course of a decade and a half, through three more books of poetry (*Kashmir, Protuberances*, and *The Book of Things*), a fictional travelogue in Peru (*January in the Middle of Summer*), and a collection of lyric essays (*Berlin*), which received the 2007 Rožančeva Award for the best book of essays written in Slovenian. The philosophical and lyrical sophistication of his poems, along with his work as a leading book editor and festival organizer, earned for Šteger a reputation that quickly traveled beyond the borders of Slovenia. The international reach of his work seems appropriate considering its international concerns and refusal to acknowledge limits to, or boundaries of, art, thought, or genre. Although grounded in and growing from his hometown of Ptuj, Šteger's work in multiple genres, and on many fronts, testifies to his growing stature as one of Central Europe's most essential literary figures.

Šteger's fourth book, *Knjiga Reči* (*The Book of Things*), is the ideal introduction to his work for English readers. Published in Slovenia in 2005, the book consists of 50 poems—a proem ("A") followed by seven sections of seven poems each. The book's careful architecture is reflected in the poems themselves, most of which are composed in couplets, tercets, or quatrains, a departure from Šteger's largely stanzaless poems in his previous books. The "things" explicitly treated in the book include the high and the low, the natural and the artificial, the mundane and the unlikely. Objects of all stripes are transformed by Šteger's alchemy. Though various and variously treated, the things in *The Book of Things* have in common the attention of a singular mind.

The poet's perspective—omniscient yet intimate, detached yet obsessive— allows him to delve into the prehistory and parallel lives of things, as when he muses on the growth rings visible in the wood of a chair, full of "the noises of centuries." Or when he transforms the dimensions of a package from centimeters to gazes, solitudes, and obsessions. Or when he views a cork as a liminal object, marking the divide between "memory" and "oblivion" while also securing "the genie of Aladdin's lamp" and "Pandora's evil spirits." But Šteger pushes even further, sometimes so far that he speculates his way toward the paradoxical or nonsensical. Cause and effect switch places, perceiver becomes perceived, and the objects somehow emerge with the upper hand.

In her essay "The Intensity of Mute Presence" ("Intenzivnost neme prisotnosti"), Lucija Stepančič notes Šteger's "provocative" approach in constructing a book from basic things and how his focus "chains us to the world of things, the ordinary, while stimulating anticipation that he must assert himself right here and now." The result of Šteger's "lightning quick perception" and ability to uncover an "unimaginable wealth of meaning" in these poems is "humbleness in that noble sense, when simplicity enhances strength." Stepančič also recognizes the book's "emotional and imaginative wealth of suggestive beauties and pleasures" and its "penetrating force" as well as the "density of details, which draw in the reader's attention like a whirlpool."

The eminent Slovenian poet Dane Zacj, in nominating *The Book of Things* for the Prešeren Fund award, notes that the things in *The Book of Things* "wait in ambush and will lash you with wry truth. . . . Through your mouth they tell the truth about themselves and your human squalor. They speak without reproaches, without moralizing. . . . The poet moves in these poems on the sharp edge of the possible and the impossible. On the edge of peril." The Slovenian philosopher and translator Gorazd Kocijančič has praised Šteger's "insatiable curiosity" in these poems as well as how the poems are "deadly serious" in their "playfulness." In his own prose, Šteger has cited the French poet Francis Ponge as an inspiration; like Ponge, Šteger has, in Maurice Blanchot's words, "gone over to the side of objects." And the poems' puzzlelike qualities and general simplicity of diction are reminiscent of the Serbian poet Vasko Popa's work. But the angles and lines are all Šteger.

Although the poems in *The Book of Things* are not formal in the conventional sense, they nevertheless carry a kind of formality that deserves to be transferred as much as possible into English. In Slovenian, the poems in *The Book of Things* employ subtle sound play, puns, doublings, and echoes, which I have tried to transmute into English on a comparable linguistic scaffolding. Of course, the ideal translation of these poems would not be other poems, but the things themselves.

—Brian Henry

THE BOOK OF THINGS

A

A died. And didn't die. Like his father
A, like his grandfather he drowned in the village graveyard.

Drowned but didn't drown. He went into the mud.
Into the mud and into the dumb stones in the mud.

Silent there now. Forgetting. Erasing. Is there now and isn't.
Because there is no place. He is without beginning and end. A-A-A.

Someone died. No one. His name—forgotten.
Like his father's and his grandfather's name. Sometimes

A a rattling of things. The one who went to bed
Sometimes gets up, the one who keeps vigil continues dying.

Sometimes A-A-A the unbearable terror of space searching for its voice.
Sometimes A-A-A the monotonous sadness of rain over streets.

A-A-A gurgles when it rolls out of the sea.
A-A-A the sigh of quartz in watches.

Surely it is only—A is dead.

Whoever thinks he sometimes hears him should listen with the other ear,
Whoever doesn't hear him will go on listening in vain.

I.

Egg

When you kill it at the edge of the pan, you don't notice
That the egg grows an eye in death.

It is so small, it doesn't satisfy
Even the most modest morning appetite.

But it already watches, already stares at your world.
What are its horizons, whose glassy-eyed perspectives?

Does it see time, which moves carelessly through space?
Eyeballs, eyeballs, cracked shells, chaos or order?

Big questions for such a little eye at such an early hour.
And you—do you really want an answer?

When you sit down, eye to eye, behind a table,
You blind it soon enough with a crust of bread.

KNOTS

There are knots whose artistry you know by heart.
And another kind that come from Smirna.

There are sisters you won't free from your memory.
And brothers, bound to you back to back.

And mothers, woven into tattered sweaters.
And fathers, tossing at night in their own traps.

For these knots are like someone
Secretly led a rope through your ear.

As if you were this rope and the knots your family.
They are not of Gordian origin and do not come from Smirna.

They are from near and far, and easily and with effort
They settled in you. A short time ago, since forever.

Be patient with your knots.
Let them grow, let them tighten in peace.

The day comes when the rope rises up in drowsy silence.
Like a fakir you climb out of your self.

STONE

No one hears what the stone keeps to himself.
Insignificant, it is only his, like pain,
Caught between the leather of a shoe and the sole.

When you slip it off, leaves spin in bare alleys.
What was, will never be again,
And piles of others are signs in decay.
The smell of nearby clinics. Mute, you go on.

What you keep to yourself, no one hears.
You are the only inhabitant of your stone.
You just threw it away.

GRATER

You remember how your mother, Jocasta,
Returned from the pigsty with a gaping palm.

Inside the madness of pain a window opened.
She stepped out and stepped out of her body.

You remember how your startled father was changing a bandage,
How, mid-escape, the edges of the bandage turned red.

This time the grater's whisper is yours. The world is being whittled away.
The apple wedge is getting smaller, but who is there for whom?

Are you merely an instrument of the apple in your palm?
Silently it grates you, a ripe buddhist, idared samsara.

When it vanishes you, you open your eyes, like your mother
That time, on the other side of the wound.

CAT

Custodian of whose stone, whose breeze in his hair?
A smirking sphinx, a castrated transvestite in a fur.
When he lifts his tail, he still steers the sides of a cursed sky.
A skeptic cautiously preserving the world with reverie.

He avoids bad weather, unknown pants legs, membership in political
     parties.
He'd rather sprawl like a mobster shot on a staircase,
In a cathedral of afternoon light, near the chirruping of angels,
Or he curls into the fluff between rings of space and time.

He allows himself to be stroked only twice.
He knows that people have more dogs than love.
When he closes his eyes, he falls through the barking in your heart.
When he opens them, gold dust sprays out as out of cracked amphoras,

Which lie too deep even for divers with the longest breath.

SAUSAGE

Did you see? Two hundred thousand frankfurters
Demonstrated for workers' rights.

Six million kosher salami gassed in the second world war
And a million hot sausages murdered fifty years later in the Balkans.

But at the same time, concern. The number of obese mortadella is rising.
It is necessary to take immediate steps against gonorrhea in the blood
        sausage.

And ooooh, some special sausage in a mini skirt.
And look at that Hungarian in high heels. Her stitch and wonderbra.

Meaty mixture of lies, fears, faltering and hope.
But why love, this frightening concept?

Is your stomach rumbling again? Come, put it in your mouth.
Between the anus and the mouth the appetite of a body for a body.

Bulimic mass, caught in the bowel of language.
Hurt it. Take it. Let the words burst between your teeth.

Urinal

The backs of male shadows amidst the stink of urine.
Like some firing squad, staring
At the multiplying ceramic tiles.

The wall stretches out in front of you, too.
A fish is pushing her white head through
From the other side, doesn't penetrate.

She wants to drink up the whole world, which she carries,
To release the surplus human weight.
Who knows, perhaps she already did so long ago.

And aren't the faces of the men urinating
Reflections of Jonah's, squeezed between fishy spikes?
What is here, what there?

What kind of human voice is on the other side of the urinal?
Are people happier, more timeless there, fish Fa?
Or there is no other side,

Only the visions of drunks, tensed in fear
That you don't close your thirsty mouth, Faronika,
As fair punishment for grinding your yellowed teeth,

And castrate us.

II.

CHOCOLATE

He died in order to be a bar of chocolate in front of you.
He wishes that you too would consume the anguish of his death.

Limitlessly. That fear and deliverance would melt in your mouth.
His sweet entrails, the bitter curves of his concoctions.

He asks you to unwrap him, to reveal yourself in the proper light.
Beyond kindness. Beyond mercy and forgiveness.

The two of you touch wordlessly, in the tongue of mute gifts.
What you break and eat, breaks and feeds on you.

Your saliva, the secret feeling of an empty mouth is his.
Your fingers, which search for him in drawers. But not the reverse.

You must remain hungry so that god can still give.
And what your god once gave, he endlessly takes.

Raisins

Whose veins, whose loves, whose traces,
Whose time evaporated in the wrinkles of raisins.

The cool grains of past summers. You eat them and you eat.
As you would eat the fingertips of god, who holds all.

Reduced to the utter humility of the aged.
Like handfuls of pensioners on a religious trip.

They rise from the table and plunge into your roof.
The whole bunch rises. Truly rises.

Whose arteries, whose fears, whose traces,
Whose gargling you gulp down with the wrinkles of raisins.

The aged fingers grab you from within,
Choking you until you spit out their name.

SHOVEL

The workers left. Your best friend
Stopped alone in the middle of a half-scraped plot.
As if she would want to work without a break.

She already dug up so much of the world, not seeing
That the soil does not end beneath the soil
And that the deeper the dig, the harder it is for a little shovel.

Will she dig up some insight?
Butterflies' bones, coins of saliva, the tongue of a mute?
Is her calling her only purpose?

So that she distracts herself on quiet evenings,
Like one who stares at the thickening darkness through a window,
Which stares through the thickening darkness in oneself.

HAT

Who lives under the hat?
Under the hat, which are three?
Three hats.

Three, which are one.
When brows meet.
When brims twist blackly.

In the midst of distant music
A black ribbon and plume flutter.
Guess! Guess!

Under which does a little hope crouch?
Under whom does hollow fear grow?
Where is half the world hidden?

The first half thinks you.
The second is on the side of oblivion.
The third dreams the other two.

Three halves of one hat.
None changes the mind beneath him.
Only the heads are changed.

Three heads, three hats.
They spin slowly into dawn.
You uncover. One alone.

ANT

It clings to objects tenaciously.
They shift about slowly, it moves with them,
Like the invisible moving through the visible world.

Hair for a blade. A beetle's body for wheat grain. Trace for trace.
So it rises, what you call home.
The border between the safety of tunnels and the unbearable expanse.

It returns from far away, always by the same way.
And it brings no messages. And no prophecies.
A period at the end of an increasingly intricate clause.

And there aren't names for what it is.
When it disappears into its maze, only hope remains
That at least there are names for what it isn't.

UMBRELLA

In the afternoon he rises from the silence in the corner.
Smiling mercifully like Saint Sebastian.

When he takes your palm, the world turns on itself.
Outside he unbuttons his too-tight tuxedo.

You step inside him as into a childhood lair.
You duck among the arrows that pierce his ribcage.

The sheltering shadow swallows up rain clouds.
As if stones would drip from the ground, drizzle on his skin.

The arrows groan if they touch the brow of the one walking among them.
Then the pain is sweet. Then it is sexy to be a martyr.

He suffers gladly, so that you don't have to fall into the sky.
He indulges in your pressure when cars drive past.

You stop and listen to the blunt booms between his ribs.
Beating like the ventricles of two hundred pedophiles before an infarct.

Although it is cool. Cool and tight.
And there is no heart. No internal organs.

As if amidst nothing nothing extends to the body.
As if knives would slide inside the surface of the wind.

Sometimes he borrows your mouth for his own quackish voice.
You open them like fish then, but it is not prayer that comes out.

Gargling. Stuttering. Mumbling.
As if someone were drowning in your head in his chest in your palm.

Finally he bursts out laughing.
At which, at whose end?

The sky watches you blackly from puddles.
You will go there, from where heaven climbs wetly along your trouser leg.

BREAD

Every time, he leads you into temptation to become a gentleman
Who feeds on crumbs under his servant's table.

He asks you to do him harm, for you to stab him,
To shred him to pieces, consume his still warm body.

Without shame he appears to you naked as at Creation.
He is a pervert. He provokes you with abstinence.

But he is being given you and you give. And every morning
And every evening you repeat the floury game.

He made you into a crematory of guilt.
When he feeds you, you speak and instantly are more famished.

Yes, yes, he loves you, that is why he accepts your knife.
He knows that all his wounds crumble in your hands.

III.

Doormat

Who are you, where do you come from, with whom do you walk to visit?
In her eyes your time is running in place.

That is why she forgives footsteps gone astray.
Forgives the lame, the rash, the drunk.

He who crosses over her cheek is not a trespasser.
She wipes your feet in her hair.

Wipes your name in hers. Until it is untranslatable.
She is not here to disclose directions. She is not there to reveal the way.

She accepts you as part of the scenery from which you come.
As part of the scenery into which you disappear.

Her hair sometimes wakes you with a tickle.
Then pure dirt flakes from words.

A voice clears its throat from traveling silently.
But she overtakes him: *Enter in peace. Enter in peace.*

She loves the invisible passages between questions.
What hurts, falls through her. The answer is always love.

HAND DRYER

Who speaks when you are not speaking in your own name?
When you do not pretend to speak in the name of another,
But there is the presence of a voice like the ghost's at a séance?
Just *retro larifari, cadabra abra, aha, aha, blah blah?*

It happens, as if the wind would speak through you.
As if the bora speaks, the *Košava*, the *Passat*, icy Siberian winds.
It happens, invisible while speaking in a clear voice.
And they do not happen. Their returns bring no changes.

Or indeed, somewhere between, where the living brush against the dead.
Drops, with which you have sprinkled their brow, evaporate from your
        palms.
Again you press the silver button on the plastic box.
Again they come roaring, this time to warm your frigid fingers.

Just *abracadabra, aha, aha, blah blah.* Because they bring nothing new.
The gas station toilet is just like before.
And you, too, were not changed. Only through your palms did something
        blow.
You do not hold him, but sometimes he holds you. He has your life lines.
        Your handshake.

He has no name, he who speaks when you do not speak in your name.
And no home. And no things of his own.
A no-name without a body, always on the road.
And his paths can also be yours, but yours can never be his.

Soap

You also try to retain
What has, before you caught it,
Slipped from your hands.

Your rib cage does not understand
That years limp with a crumbling knee,
That you are your own breed only during a fall.

Below and still lower alternate.
The blows are silent and insidious
And leave no bruises.

That is why some fasten themselves
To their bit of soap
With a gold chain.

Or they lock up their soapy hands
In a guarded vault
And turn the key three times.

But nothing helps.
Before you notice,
Soap slips from your hands.

The paper in which it slept
Brings misfortune to him who unwraps it.
Nothing helps.

Because your ear does not correctly comprehend.
Because your eye speaks unintelligible tongues.
Because your nose pushes you along a false trail.

That is why they call you son of a bitch,
Brother of a vagabond puppy,
A scoundrel with dirty paws.

And they happily add, that in the world
That gives once and takes endlessly,
No one remains pure of hand.

In spite of this
All the luck of this world
Has lathered between your palms.

And only now, when you rinse her, do you know
What it means to live like a dog
And to fall asleep with a smile on your muzzle.

STOMACH

What does the clerk of the stomach say?
That yesterday he was seen crossing the street.
That he didn't pay the toothpick at the restaurant.
That he is flying too high and sooner or later it will befall him.

What do the veal steak and two flasks of teran say?
That the light suddenly ran out.
That it grew tight and stuffy, though you still didn't leave.
That it is sad when you drop so low.

What does the thigh, which grazes behind the cow's head, say?
That his gross worth grows with every morsel.
That he will enter the souls of fifteen wedding guests and two dogs
          simultaneously.
That it isn't cold as long as there's enough grass and roads on the horizon.

And what does this gurgle, this drooling stutter whisper to you?
That it isn't cold as long as there's enough meat and potatoes.
That it is sad when you drop so low.
That all creatures which fly sooner or later will fall.

PUPA

The growing presence of the butterfly in her
Does not fill her with fear.
She hangs in her cocoon world like some religious fanatic,
And this world inside another, larger cocoon.
Through this cocoon you walk home.

Your step seems firmly pressed into time,
But in truth you recognize only the pins
With which small tortoiseshell, admiral, peacock
Are impaled on the wall.
Your ignorance only grows.

How many cocoons enclose the last one?
When do seconds die?
In whose sleep do clouds arise?
Isn't it insignificant, the likelihood
That one day we will fly away?

KNIVES

They hang there freshly sharpened.
In the glimmering light. Light.

The butcher's shop is a big family enterprise.
Two million butchers and customers.

Customers and butchers. You hardly discern them.
For some are others. And others are others.

The buyer puts on the blood-stained apron.
The butcher opens a purse for a still twitching shoulder.

The knives watch you coldly, with closed eyes.
They remember where they were, what they mediated.

If you grab them, you feel a slight shiver in the handles.
At dusk the blades reflect the deaths into which they were thrust.

But where are the bones? Where are the names?
Look, look, they are also stuck in your throat.

And when you speak, you also speak with the silence of the murdered.
They are stuck in your duodenum.

And when you need to go, you shit what was slaughtered before your birth.
They are scattered in your shallow chest.

And when you get off in haste after urgent business,
It is not cans and brushwood that crack under your feet.

Where are they? Where are they? Where are they?
Everyone knows about them. No one remembers.

COAT

Do you remember the archivist who committed suicide
Because of one misplaced sheet?
The three librarians who never returned from the warehouse?

The history students who bit the professor's neck in an exam
Because he could not remember the price of potato soup in May 1889?
The parrot who endlessly shouted *Stalingrad, sexual revolution, self-reliance*?

But there is another memory, with which you hold nothing.
The coat, which no one made, which no one can own.
But which you can borrow, so you can be warm and daydream.

A guest in your own home. A tenant of the second person.
With the first memory you try in vain to remember it all.
You rarely think of the second, which calls you out of nothing.

IV.

JELLY

Some were on their way through Tivoli,
In the middle of gymnastics on rings,
In the middle of lion taming at the circus
When bones leaped out of their shoulders.

Others got greasy fingers while making deals.
Small bones spurted from their palms.
Knuckles were bent by the pressure
Like sealing wax.

Left under desks and altars, vertebrae pooled.
Astonished heads collapsed into themselves
Like wet paper sacks.
Teeth dangled in the middle of a sentence.

Dialects evaporated discreetly.
Then amoebae, bacteria and algae began to multiply
Until jelly flooded the streets.
Whoever touched someone stuck to him forever.

BANDAGE

Every morning she covers your head. And presses, presses.
Owing no one, you must pay everyone.

But not like the wounded one at the front. No one turns his head after you.
And not like someone who smacks against the doorjambs of confessionals.

Silently and slowly the sky collapsed on you
So that you alone do not know, why your bandage.

You grope for her. You search. You try to take her off, you tear,
Because you do not know if she is hiding a wound, if she hides anything.

Your fingers stretch into the void, become tangled, like politicians.
Your thoughts just accumulate new knots in the head.

Like women who go home with jugs on their heads,
You wander the globe with your bandage.

But the fountains dried out long ago.
Without borders you have nowhere to go.

MINT

Mintafiction, minthane, mintabolism.
There the smell of mint grows out of bone,
Out of a neighbor's thumb and a stranger's shin.
No animal could do it, it's not worth repeating.

Mintatax, mintasound, mintaphysics.
For what stays, when only plants try
To heal a musician's rib and the mayor's skull.
No laxative could do it, it's not worth mentioning.

Even less who will remember, cannot forget
Endless fields of mint, ruts, indifference.
Mintamen. Mintanight. Mintanaught.
No dictionary could do it, it's not worth noting.

SHOES

They protect you
So the road presses softly on you.
Messengers that swish between you
And the world of trails that erase each other.
Made out of skin and sutures.
And yours are stitched from the words *skin and sutures*.
Protect them.
You can be naked and without anything,
But with shoes on your feet you will never be poor,
Never remain hidden,
Knocked down under a bed,
Abandoned in an armoire, forgotten in an attic.
Sleep with them.
Bathe in the shoes,
Make love with them on.
Let them always warn you
That you are only here on a brief visit.
Soon you will have to walk on.
Never take them off.
When you take them off, the journey will have ended.
They bury you like a gypsy,
Barefoot and without a name.

Sea Horse

Creatures of liquid light, vagabonds of underwater currents,
Students of belly dancing, the ocean's brides loyal to his moods.

With their final breath, forgotten Phoenician gods
Inflated glassy bodies that shine like empty clepsydrae.

Tails wrap playfully around the mesh in fishing nets,
The tiny wings' fluttering sketches pillows of eternity in the restless sleep
    of the drowned.

They are princes of confidence. And when the female spawns eggs into
    the male
So that he bears them and gives birth, they are the social democratic ideal
    of reproduction.

Too fragile for guilt, but noticeable enough
That the jealous eye of the blue mussel thinks of beauty and love.

Among the shadows of people, sea horse bodies dry,
Lose translucence, become rough and blunt.

Between two fingers you crush them, beauty and love,
Into what is not beautiful and what (you don't remember when) stopped
    loving.

SALIVA

Not just birth, and copulation and death.
Birth, copulation death.

There is also spitting. After all, everywhere, always.
The marking of death and stirring the dead.

Lazarus rise. Lazarus sit down. Lazarus rise. Lazarus sit down.
It regenerates in your mouth.

It pours, this poisonous, sweet force.
Between teeth, when you spit your own little genocide.

You push it with the tongue. Pour resin over it, phlegm of words.
Him, who raises into birth. Into copulation.

And him, who sits down into *s*. Who sits down.
Who slips to an unknown place, so that you swallow deeply.

You hiss, for you know each other inside out.
He lurks in the mirror. Waits to spit in your face.

TOOTHPICK

A bit of undigested meat has gotten lost
And is calling for a revolt.

Rebellious foreign body. It signals from your mouth.
Although you do not speak.

Although you allowed no one to speak
In your name.

But it keeps yelling,
Incites an uprising, applies pressure.

You try to remove it with the tongue,
But there are no words that would silence its protest.

A little Robespierre in Polyphemus' mouth.
But without sly fortune, without gods and flocks on his side.

You extract him from your conscience, grind what is gnawing you.
Down with the revolution.

Although the last linden falls.
You sprawl on her stump, break off a splinter and belch.

The toothpick juts from your mouth like a centurion's spear,
Which cleansed the empire.

The black hole in the tooth whispers:
This kingdom also will collapse on itself one day.

V.

WINDOW

Sometimes it lies in your lap and sips you.
Sometimes it mirrors you only with its right eyeball. Snakily.

At night it disappears. Then you notice someone lean through what
      disappeared
And vomit all the hours, all the scenes on you.

You never come closer to him than to the space that he mirrors.
He breeds your curiosity with scenes that you cannot digest.

The blinds carve his abdomen into thin slices.
Only what goes still behind emotions sometimes reassembles them into
      afternoon light.

The gift and the punishment of drafty gods. Close it! Close it,
So these clouds also don't crash on you.

SALT

Beware the ruler's dialectics.
The choice between Krpan the slaughterer and Brdavs the martyr is false.

No politics and no messianics.
You don't command army bunks, don't raise the dead with a stretcher.

That's why you shouldn't speak just half.
How to halve dew, infatuation, time?

Let this, which was entrusted to you, arrive whole.
Neigh, Kobilica, Rocinante, St. George's white Pegasus.

Transport your cargo tirelessly.
Precipices open up beneath your hoofs.

Speak, but don't tell a story that others call yours.
It is as insignificant as an abandoned salt mine.

Someone smuggles back through its dark shafts
What was seized from the sea.

Help him.

CORK

He was extracted from a tree, ground and made anew
To protect access to mystery like the last seraph.

You never know which side he's on.
On the side of memory, on the side of oblivion.

He guards the world from the genie of Aladdin's lamp,
Closes firmly so that Pandora's evil spirits don't flee.

Or is evil already on this side from the beginning
And does the cork protect the last refuge of silence?

Anyhow. The fat innkeeper's fingers drilled him, pulled,
And pushed again with the bloody side turned to you.

What was stored in safety escaped.
It swooshed down the throat like emptiness into the bottle.

The cork in her mouth still bleeds.
And still silent, you swallow.

The voices of fugitives from neighboring tables grow distant,
The consolation of the bottle, that the message in her didn't travel in vain.

WINDSHIELD WIPERS

Both of them hide something,
That is why they move in such harmony.
Like two serfs in black rubber boots.
They get up to go immediately back to bed.

Bits of mud. Drops. Drops. Insects smeared.
They wipe but cannot erase.
Because there is no one who could grant them the power of absolution.
Their goal of clear vision is complete delusion.

No one frees himself following the world's flashes.
They slip over the windshield to an unknown place.
Your guilt is transparent. Watertight. Inspected.
When it bursts into dust you forget you exist.

TAPEWORM

It's not important, bud or pollen, vagina or penis.
Everyone puts on a pink jacket or a blue sweater
And gets dirty during rose graftings and car washings.

Under the stretched edge of the exposed belly
(Did beer fertilize? Did the unwanted two bulge?)
The little tapeworm sleeps twisted like a Möbius strip.

Sleep peacefully, little tapeworm.
The world outside is cold and famished,
But you procreate via your solitude.

The only impediment to your own repetitions,
You suck on a staggering daydream about the body that hosts you.
Sleep calmly. No one masters even half of one's fate.

Some decide for a bud or a penis.
The man lifts his skirt and the woman draws her breeches.
But it's another thing to be the friend of one's own tapeworm.

Some starve their own mouths to the last word,
Stuff them with sauerkraut on an empty stomach
To expel you.

It's horrible, the writing of your suction cups,
Secret signs saying you are both male and female,
That the border between you and the world is one alone.

It's horrible, this quiet sipping inside,
A reminder that no one wished to be a girl or a boy,
But only warm and safe.

Bud or pollen? Vagina or penis?
While dancing, the pants chafe the woman's thighs
And the man rips his garters and his left breast pops.

So just sleep safely, sleep peacefully, sleep like you would sleep
Between the words, which wrote neither pollen nor vagina,
But daydreamers and parasites.

HAYRACK

Guardian of the land.
Guardian of the land's inhabitants.
Guardian of their consciences.
When everyone sleeps, the hayrack pays attention
So that no one slips away from the game,
Misses the return of King Matjaž.

Slovenian heroes sacrificed their lives
So their sons could freely dry
The contents of their skulls
In the Alpine breeze of the hayrack's rungs.
The vast meadows are their souls.
Cows chew and shit them
And out of cow shit their souls grow
Still more beautiful and succulent.

Oh, hayrack, *yes*, hayrack.

No one knows who was the first to build bridges,
Who knitted the first walkways,
Raised the first carrier pigeon,
Invented the doorknob and opened a neighbor's door.
But only a Slovene could construct
A prison in the middle of open country,
A cage that divides the world:
On one side hypocrisy,
On the other a chronically inflamed prostate.

Hayrack. Hayyyyrack. Hay-raaaa-ck.

Your mother, insanity,
Squeezes you to herself when you are sad and yearn.
She lets you eat edges and drink morphield.
Because it is nothing. Don't be afraid. Don't cry, she tells you.

The enemy is constantly everywhere,
But he cannot get to you as long as
Brigadiere Hayrackino, Hauptmann Hayracker,
Ezredes Häyräckek and Pukovnik Hayrakić protect you.

You sigh.

In the distance, mountains.
In overcoats, moths.
In the poem, gold.

You sneeze.

You scratch under your navel and know:
Together you will make it.

WHEELBARROW

It lies tipped over at the edge of a slope.
The wheel turns, blinded in the wind.

A mouth vomited like after chemotherapy.
Now already whispering again, but without relief.

It isn't a Homeric hero. It has the stomach of a clumsy ram
That smuggled something larger and heavier than itself.

All to this point, where their trace goes silent
And it must outwit the gaze, outwit the word.

Cargo begins to gather back uphill.
The wounds heal, as if they are only on paper.

VI.

TRUMPET

The internal and external side of the breath make knots
Four times between the pointer and ring finger.

The cheek puffs up in a grotesque grimace.
(Did the creator look like this before the creation?

And from where the need to gauge the sound of emptiness?)
The knots in the fist are quietly stretched so they cover the view.

When the first tears, one hears a quiet fart of fear.
When the second tears, one hears a chuckling rogue.

When the third tears, from the father's trumpet rush
Trenches, elephants, wedding guests, two dancers, Trotamora, a radio.

A mighty noise floods the world. It's not good all together.
No, it's not good all together. On the last try it must succeed.

When you blow the fourth time, the trumpet cracks mutely. Is someone
    set free?
But how. Only the father's radio gets a little loud.

POTATO

The potato remembers the soil better than the farmer who digs him out,
     his nightmares.
Inside his forehead you are born from the fallow and you eat back his
     potato.

It's better to have a head buried deep in clay and to keep silent
By the anus, temperate against the sky, than to repeat the ancient tale of
     torment.

It's better to forget that your legs and stomach dangle in emptiness.
Lucky that your hands don't know they are held only by a few peelings—
     the last land.

When you submerge him at the bottom of the pot, you revive the ancient
     curse.
The eye of Atahualpa prophesies bad luck as it is pulled out.

Centuries, which separate you, passed by more quickly, as the Colorado
     beetle spawns.
His time is yet to come, and you are running out of potato.

Earring

The whole time he tells you what to do.
His voice is chocolate candy filled with hysteria.

He is a loving blackmailer. An owl blind in one eye.
It is enough that he sees half the world to command the other half.

He gladly inspects himself in the mirror, but goes crazy if you praise him
Before another. He is not your property. He is not your adornment.

Only when you dance and when you make love with him, he coos.
Then cages open. Then he is the white message bearer of the gods.

Gradually you detach him more often, hide him in a box, misplace him.
But his bite at the lobe still whispers to you.

As if Eros holds you with invisible filigree pliers
And solders words of guilt and the silence of betrayal into your ear.

A copy of a stone from Sisyphus' mountain is set inside it.
You roll hope uphill. And you roll downhill drunk, despondent and alone.

STROBE LIGHT

Negative selection among Red Bulls.
When it flashes on you, the dust of millennia glints on your tusks.
Fiercely your gills open and close.
You and your rivals inspect each other, waver with monkey tails.

Yet females were not delivered.
They breathe through cocktail straws on the side of life.
They wait and are switched off. Assess and are switched off.
There are no more reptiles, but still no Lilith.

You are nestless, a rock closed the entrance to your cave,
A beast on the run before its helpless prey,
Not Rilke's and not Dante's tiger.
Restless, you are suckled by fear and anticipation.

Your stride from the steppe to the dance floor is therefore awkward.
But then it somehow starts one two one two three four.
Drum beats rush into the ear like the final judgment.
Light creates and erases you, creates and erases, creates and erases.

SALMON

After years of living in the ocean
Pacific salmon swim up the river
Whose current brought them down.

It takes weeks, their journey to the source,
To the place where the first eye shadowed
In featureless roe.

They do not gather more food.
They do not follow everyday survival strategies.
They do not search, do not flee, do not hunt. They are on the way.

Gradually their skin goes blood red.
Their heads turn green.
The male's mouth grows hooked and long.

Visible to all, they travel.
By jumping up waterfalls
They wound themselves to death by the thousand.

The rest swim further through rapids,
Toward the brown wavy hair, the shadow that awaits them,
Bent over the arch of their rushing world.

How delicate is the death of wild red salmon
Impaled on bear's claws.
As if death is not the end, but a mute passage.

And Destrnik is a place in the heart of Alaska.

The cub stands on the bank
And watches his mother, who has bewitched the river.
Her offspring already on his own.

Rapids, waterfalls, the deadly blows of paws.
Salmon seldom manage to return to their source,
Conclude beginning and end under their fins.

By spawning they die off slowly in icy waters.
Bloated, they spread in pools.
You walk against the current, which takes them. Which takes you.

SHIT

Children happily rummage through him for a sign.
Provence's princesses made compresses
Of eternal youth with him.
In the spring he is scattered on fields and corn grows.

At a sharp pain you look back happy.
But it is not shit that you see, that looks at you.
Your muddy soul climbed out of you.
Your only true child. He fell from you.

Without a soul you are form without value.
That is why you lose it and create. Lose and create.
You do not exchange your shit for gold.
You exchange your shit only for love.

Paper Clip

You put down the paper confused.
You only now notice the rusty imprint of a paper clip.
A spiral sign for the way inward.

She held together scraps of the world like an invisible thread.
She warmed you, so enveloped in herself. Like a fetus.
Like a snail. Like a body in a mass grave.

Her intention is not to add or take away from the world.
Not a creator, the little paper clip. She only causes contact.
Someone removed her. Who, why—you don't know.

Nor how many sheets were lost.
With a finger you go over the trace and start to read again.
Before you opens a space within a space within a space.

This poem has no end.

VII.

ASPIRIN

It's enough. Otherwise no, you didn't expect
That it would end now, in such a way, but it's enough.

You will dissolve between thoughts watching you more inanely,
Between words, which concealed no one's silence.

This is nothing fatal. Your departure will be quiet and inconspicuous.
No rooster will take off, no one will sneeze behind you.

It will just rustle in some corner, as if water were poured on aspirin.
A white coin from Noah's ark tossing in a glass.

Her passengers and messages won't last.
Particles of the pill will dissolve like cypress wood.

The secret of life is not to remain the same. The same. The same.
The secret of life is that you rustle. Shhhh.

Enough. It's enough. Drink from your poverty. Until empty.
You won't escape with hemlock or some other ruse.

No one ferries you. No one will be saved.
Only thirst will be appeased. At least for the moment.

WALL

Not a day goes by when you don't think
That a wall was put between you and the world.
Took your perspective. Banished you.

Not a morning goes by when you don't swear
That today you will tear down this wall, and not an evening
When you don't return torn down. Your revolt is meaningless.

There is no one who will grant you the security of an opposite.
Bricks are shifting alone, softly like hours.
They let you through, before the palm touched them.

Even though there is no other side, no other place.
You arrive nowhere and nothing holds you anywhere.
You are without a wall, where all this would end.

And your wall is *nowhere no one never.*

BED

So much bile, boiling blood, bitter spit, Ljubljanica, urine
Poured over just one bed.

Yes. Yes. Yes. Because. Because. Only. And no other way.

All the greenery must be educated to reproduce enfenced.
Because only a fence grows more orderly than kohlrabi.

Yes. Yes. Yes. Which. Which. So. And no other way.

Every spring kohlrabi becomes more embittered from incest.
Her head dug into the mud would eat up every soul.

Well. Well. Well. Yet is not. Though. Although. And no other way.

In autumn some roll by mistake into the neighboring bed.
The cow eats them, turns her eyes toward the cloud in herself and expires.

Oh. Oh. Ah. Ah. How. But better so than otherwise.

The death of the pregnant animal is cruel, but better, believe,
That nothing moos, as in the neighbor's bed too, in yours but only one.

This but no. No and no. Never. And no other way.

Parcel

It traveled from afar only to test you.
Two by three by six centimeters, with no addressee.

Why did your name wrap itself in silence
As if abducted in a parcel, mouth taped?

Two gazes by three solitudes is six obsessions.
Six chances divided by day and night—roughly infinite.

But perhaps No One's name is in the parcel
And yours is the inner side of the fold, which envelops it?

If you observe it from outside, you can guess, but you do not know.
If you open it, you can stammer ragged vocals, but you do not compose.

COCKER SPANIEL

Like some swine wallowing in a deadly seizure
While her red hair flows from the skull and pours over the body.

The smell of barbeque returns her again to the living.
The tail nervously deducts eternities while gobbling.

Who can digest so much affection
And not bark? Vau vau! She is probably Korean.

An Easterner in any case, judging by her concept of property
When she sits on your feet, to force a palm.

Pet her once more and prove that you love her
More than the resurrection of the pork chop in front of you.

That all this frippery of jealousy is redundant.
That the palm, which was abandoned, will never abandon her.

CHAIR

The rings in it make time look aside.
It recalls you, when you were still a primate. On all fours.
And current sapiens.
Drunk, tormented, desperate. On all fours.
A human with the perspective of floors. Of you.

It wears anal histories.
The leather skirt of a Roman centurion has warmed it.
And a few scraps on the naked buttocks of a serf.
The stiff flaxen pants of SS Senior Storm Leader
And the prancing edge of sticky miniskirts.

It knows as many stories as backsides.
But even the fronts got lost. Drifted away in rough waters.
So be grateful that it has accepted you as you are.
That it bears you. Now, when at last all is behind you,
You can entrust it with your weight, lean a head,

Slightly confused from the noises of centuries. You snore.

CANDLE

When someone dies, it is not day not night.
And no one present. Not here not there.
A small flicker above the gas stove.

Unimportant. And it does not live and did not die,
What you conceal with the palm.
It does not ask, does not give answers.

It is not on the side of good. It is not on the side of evil.
It does not know lies, not truth, not sense or nonsense.
It is not the future and not the past.

It is and at the same time is not. Is not that it is or was not you.
It will not be by itself or something else.
Not air not fire. Not light not flame.

Not abyss not hope. Not yes not no.
When someone dies, someone has not died yet.
He climbed down the wick inside himself.

You reach behind and extinguish him.

"Urinal": Fa is a popular brand of soap in Europe. Faronika is a mythologi-
cal fish common in old Slovenian folk songs. Faronika carries the world on
its back, and when there is too much evil in the world, Faronika will dive
into the cosmic sea and thus destroy the world.

"Knives": The population of Slovenia is two million. After World War II,
the Communists killed 15,000 Slovenians, who'd been stopped in Austria
by British troops and returned to Tito's partisans.

"Jelly": Tivoli is the main park in Ljubljana, Slovenia. Cf. Jakob von Hod-
dis' "Weltende."

"Mint": In Slovenian, "meta" means "mint." The poem plays on the corre-
spondence between "mint" and the prefix "meta-."

"Saliva": Cf. T. S. Eliot's "Fragment of an Agon."

"Salt": In the Slovenian folk tale "Martin Krpan" (later adapted by Fran
Levstik), the Slovenian peasant and salt smuggler Martin Krpan is called
to the Austrian court in order to defeat the evil Turkish giant Brdavs, a
personification of 'the Eastern threat.' Krpan succeeds by cutting down
the queen's most beloved linden tree and making a club. The angry queen
refuses to pay Krpan what the king had promised, but Krpan's subsequent
anger convinces the court to offer him whatever he wants. He simply asks
for permission to transport salt with Kobilica, his tiny horse. The poem
reverses the roles of Brdavs and Krpan.

"Hayrack": King Matjaž is a figure in Slovenian mythology (derived from
the Hungarian king Matthias Corvinus, 1458–1490) who sleeps with his
army hidden in the Peca mountain, destined to awake and liberate his
country. "The land" in the poem ("dežela") is also a pejorative term for
Slovenia due to a 1980s-era promotion slogan for the country: "Dobrodošli v
deželi." The hayrack is a common Slovenian tourist symbol. "[M]orphield"
is a neologism corresponding with the neologism "travmal" in the original

text; "travmal" combines the Slovenian word for "grass" with the name of a popular analgesic (Tramal). The military figures near the end of the poem are imaginary colonels from the four countries that border Slovenia—Italy, Austria, Hungary, Croatia.

"Trumpet": Trotamora is, literally, a "nightmare killer" or a "killing nightmare." Trotamora is often placed at a baby's cradle to ward off bad dreams and spirits. It is also a demon in Slovenian mythology.

"Potato": The potato was introduced to Europe via the Incas. Atahualpa, the last Inca emperor, was tortured before being killed by the Spanish. In Slovenian, to run out of potato is to run out of luck.

"Salmon": Destrnik is a small village in eastern Slovenia.

"Wall": Cf. Constantin Cavafy's "Walls."

"Bed": The Ljubljanica is the river that runs through Ljubljana, the capital of Slovenia.

ACKNOWLEDGMENTS

Bomb: "Jelly";
Boston Review: "Sea Horse";
Cincinnati Review: "Aspirin," "Chair," "Cork," "Parcel," "Pupa," "Window";
Circumference: "Coat";
Connotation: "Cocker Spaniel";
Copper Nickel: "Knots";
Crazyhorse: "Saliva," "Tapeworm";
Denver Quarterly: "Knives";
Guernica: "Earring";
New American Writing: "Hat," "Mint," "Shoes";
The New Yorker: "Grater";
Ninth Letter: "Candle";
North American Review: "Wheelbarrow";
Parthenon West Review: "Ant," "Cat," "Strobe Light," "Trumpet";
Poetry International: "Bread," "Potato," "Raisins," "Sausage";
Poetry London (UK): "Cat," "Toothpick," "Window";
Poetry Review (UK): "Ant";
A Public Space: "Windshield Wipers";
Subtropics: "Egg," "Stomach";
Times Literary Supplement: "Shovel";
TriQuarterly: "Bandage," "Salmon";
Washington Square: "A";
Zoland Poetry: "Paper Clip," "Wall."

About the Author

Aleš Šteger has published five books of poetry, a novel, and two books of essays in Slovenian. He received the 1998 Veronika Prize for the best Slovenian poetry volume of the year, the 1999 Petrarch Prize for young European authors, and the 2007 Rožančeva Award for the best book of essays written in Slovenian. His work has been translated into fourteen languages, including German, Czech, Croatian, Hungarian, and Spanish. He is a founding editor of the Beletrina publishing house, and he founded the Medana Days of Poetry and Wine festival. *The Book of Things* is his first book translated into English.

About the Translator

Brian Henry has published six books of poetry, most recently *Wings Without Birds*. His translation of Tomaž Šalamun's *Woods and Chalices* appeared from Harcourt in 2008. He has coedited *Verse* since 1995 and has received numerous awards and fellowships for his poetry and translations. He lives in Richmond, Virginia.

9 781934 414415